GW00729200

30130 074343681

Green Favours

A play

Frank Vickery

Samuel French–London
New York-Toronto-Hollywood

GREEN FAVOURS

First performed by the Sherman Theatre Company,
Cardiff at the Sherman Theatre on the 20th January,
1993 with the following cast:

Valerie	Menna Trussler
Tom	Frank Vickery

Directed by Phil Clark
Designed by Jane Linz Roberts
Lighting by Nick Macliammoir

CHARACTERS

Tom   (early forties)
Valerie (early to mid-fifties)

Other plays by Frank Vickery published by
Samuel French Ltd:

After I'm Gone
All's Fair
Breaking the String
Erogenous Zones
Family Planning
A Night on the Tiles
A Night Out
One O'Clock from the House
Spanish Lies
Split Ends
Trivial Pursuits

GREEN FAVOURS

A small wooden shed on an allotment. A terribly wet and windy morning in April around 11.10 a.m.

In addition to general gardening equipment there is a tea-chest DL of the door, and a cluster of bean sticks standing in a tin barrel behind the door. Tom's coat is hanging on one of the sticks. There is a large box, a pot on the floor in one corner, and shelves with plastic cups of runner beans, several packets of seeds and a small transistor radio

As the Curtain *rises, a rather loud thunder clap is heard, followed immediately by Tom Jones singing "It's Not Unusual". The singing moves from the auditorium and into the transistor radio. Tom is standing in the middle of the shed, brushing his teeth to the music. Realizing the tube of toothpaste is now empty, he throws it into the pot on the floor. Having finished brushing, he returns the toothbrush to the shelf. He opens the door and spits outside. He comes back into the shed and is wiping his mouth with the cuff of his shirt when he spots Valerie through the window. He quickly switches off the radio, then kneels (facing front) and begins to spray the plastic cups of runner beans*

Valerie quickly taps on the shed window before opening the door to come in, immediately closing it behind her. She has a bag with a flask in it, which she set down by the tea-chest

Valerie My God, it's ruff!
Tom Said the actress to the bishop. Let me take your coat.

He takes her coat and hangs it on a nail behind the door

Valerie (*laughing*) It's like a monsoon out there.
Tom It's so bad I thought perhaps you wouldn't come today.
Valerie You've got to be kidding. It'll take more than a bit of rough weather to keep *me* away from this place.

Tom There's a joke there somewhere about a bit of rough. (*He returns to his knees and proceeds to count the beans*)

Valerie What are you doing?

Tom Counting the beans.

Valerie For me?

Tom (*nodding*) Thirty-four.

Valerie That's three pounds forty, then.

Tom There should be a few sticks in the corner I don't use. (*He points to the cluster of bean sticks in the tin barrel*) They'll save you a couple of bob.

Valerie (*going to have a look at them*) Oh, thanks. (*She touches Tom's coat on the stick*) God, your coat is soaking wet.

Tom Oh, it'll dry.

Valerie I will be able to get the rest through the club though, won't I?

Tom Of course, you're a member now. You're not going to have any problems.

Valerie Did you think I'd give up?

Tom Not for a minute.

Valerie Why? I mean I am the first woman ever to be allowed into the gardening club. What was it that didn't make you doubt me?

Tom (*getting up*) You don't want to know.

Valerie Was it my total lack of femininity? Oh, don't look so embarrassed. It's never bothered me. Why are you smiling?

Tom It's never bothered me either.

There is a brief moment between them before Tom breaks away towards the bean sticks

Valerie What are you doing?

Tom Getting out your sticks. (*He places them on the floor*)

Valerie Leave them. I'm not going to be able to do anything with them in this weather. Oh .... they're not very tall. Still, Norman said he's got a few for me as well. (*She takes a better look*) No, they're not very tall, are they?

Tom They can be tied and joined. (*He dumps the last few of them* *down on the floor, his enthusiasm temporarily dampened. He picks up a well-worn piece of sand-paper and a chunk of carved wood and sits on a small box R)*

Valerie (*after a pause*) I've told Alan I think we should invest in a chest freezer. But he wants to hang on. Doesn't believe in rushing into anything. He's not going to admit it was a good idea until we're sitting down to Christmas dinner with vegetables grown by our own little fingers.

Tom If he won't let you buy a freezer there's plenty of things you can preserve. A couple of empty jars and a book from the library and you'll be away.

Valerie Oh, I plan to do all that. And if I have any luck at all with the outdoor tomatoes, we'll be eating chutney well into next year. (*Slight pause*) What's that?

Tom It's suppose to be a pear.... when it's finished. (*He holds it out to her*)

Valerie (*taking the piece of wood and looking at it*) Did you carve it?

Tom It was something to do.

Valerie It's good. (*She hands it back. Pause. She sits on the tea-chest*) Do you know ... I've only got one dress in my wardrobe?

Tom Is that suppose to mean something?

Valerie Only if you want it to.

Pause. Tom spots Val's flask in her bag

Tom Any tea in your flask?

Valerie Fancy a cup?

Tom I could murder one.

Valerie (*reaching for her bag*) I hope it's still hot. I made it early this morning.

Tom I don't suppose you've got anything to eat as well, have you?

Valerie I've brought us a pasty each, home made of course, and there's a couple of biscuits, too.

Tom Shall I help myself?

Valerie No, go on ... I'll do it. (*She hands Tom a pasty in a paper* *bag before pouring tea from the flask*) You make a start.

Tom tucks into it

What are they like?

He nods with his mouth full

Tea looks all right, anyway. There's yours. (*She hands it to him. Pause. She sits back down*) At the end of the day it all comes down to what you're comfortable in.

Tom What?

Valerie And I've always felt better in trousers.

Pause. Tom nods, realizing what she meant, before taking another bite of pasty

He wouldn't stop me having a freezer, anyway.

He looks at her

Alan. I usually end up having what I want ... one way or another. (*She gets up and looks out of the window*) It's not going to stop, is it?

Tom In for the day now, I should think.

Valerie I can see Norman's got the right idea – he's lit a fire in his shed.

Tom Are you cold?

Valerie No, I'm fine.

Tom My anorak's there. (*He points to it*)

Valerie No, I'm all right. It's OK. (*Slight pause*) I'm glad I didn't put those lettuce in yesterday. They'd have all been washed away today.

Tom You'll find you'll lose a few things anyway.

Valerie God, there's half a pond at the bottom of my plot. If it keeps up everything's going to be flooded and I'll lose the lot!

Tom No you won't. (*He goes to her*)

They both look out of the window

I've dug a trench. As soon as the water rises to a certain level it'll drain away.

Valerie When did you do that?

Tom (*after a slight pause*) This morning. (*He eases away from her, sits back down and finishes the pasty*)

Valerie Is that how your coat is still wet – digging me a trench?

Tom I dug one for myself as well.

Valerie What time did you get here then?

Tom Oh ... I don't know. Early though.

Valerie What's the matter? Helen kick you out of bed?

Tom Yeah, something like that. (*Having finished the pasty, he throws the paper bag on to the floor*)

Valerie You haven't eaten it already? The pasty.

Tom And very nice it was too.

Valerie You must be starving. Have mine – go on. (*She takes the other pasty from her bag*)

Tom No. I'm all right now.

Valerie I only want a biscuit. Have it.

Tom Are you sure?

Valerie Positive. Here you are. (*She hands it to him*)

Tom Ta.

Valerie I'd have brought more if I'd realized. (*Pause*) That coat of yours ... it's never going to dry just perched there like that. Why don't I make a dash with it and ask Norman if I can put it in front of his fire?

Tom It's not that wet.

Valerie It's soaking. Feel it for yourself. (*She feels it*)

Tom (*furiously*) Val, just leave it, OK? (*He gets up and looks out of the window again, turning his back to her*) If you want to go and spend some time with Norman, go. You don't have to have an excuse. (*He tosses the pastie away*)

Valerie I only offered to dry your coat.

Tom Yeah, of course you did.

Valerie That's all I wanted to do, Tom. What's the matter with you?

He doesn't answer

I've noticed it before, every time I bring Norman into the conversation.

Tom (*facing away from her*) I just think you've got a thing about him.

Valerie No Tom ... it's you that's got a thing, not me.

Tom You're making me sound like I'm jealous or something.

Valerie (*sitting down on the tea-chest*) You're doing a pretty good job of that yourself.

Tom (*getting his coat and throwing it to her*) Take the bloody thing then. If it means that much, take it and dry it in Norman's shed.

Valerie (*unable to believe this*) You've got it all wrong.

Tom (*turning back to the window*) Yeah, well ... take it anyway.

Valerie (*going to him and turning him around to face her*) Now look, let's get this straight. If I don't have a thing about Norman and you don't – what the hell is all this about?

Tom He's divorced – did you know?

Valerie Yes, of course I knew. I don't understand what the problem is.

Tom Oh, I think you do.

Valerie You're not making very much sense, Tom. If you're trying to say that you think there's something going on between Norman and me, then go ahead and say it. You're way out of line and completely wrong, but say it. At least I'll know which way we're going.

Tom He's not a bad-looking fella.

Valerie Neither are you, but there's nothing between us. (*Pause*) I don't treat Norman or you any different than I treat the rest of them.

Tom Don't you?

Valerie No.

Tom (*after a slight pause*) No. (*He sits down*) Maybe you're right. Maybe you do treat us all the same ... I don't know.

Valerie (*also sitting*) I try to. (*Slight pause*) I just want to get on with people. You know yourself it wasn't a popular decision to make me a member of the gardening club. As desperate as I was to get in I didn't want to upset anyone. I try very hard to like everybody. Oh God, I haven't gone over the top, have

I? A terrible thought has just occurred to me.

Tom (*smiling, getting up and putting his cup of tea down on the low shelf*) No, no, no, no. You've got nothing to worry about. The general feeling is that you're great. Just one of the boys in fact. (*He is returning the sticks to the barrel when he gets a splinter in his finger*) Ouch! (*He puts his finger in his mouth*)

Valerie What have you done?

Tom (*taking his finger out of his mouth*) A splinter, look.

She looks at his finger

Valerie I've got a safety pin in my coat, let me get it out for you. (*She gets the safety pin and goes to him*) Where is it?

He shows her. She concentrates on getting it out while Tom doesn't take his eyes off her

What about you, then? Do you think I'm one of the boys?

Tom Well ... despite everything ...

Valerie Forget I asked. I don't think I'm going to like this.

Tom Ignoring the way you wear your hair —

Valerie What's wrong with my hair?

Tom – and overlooking your grubby fingernails ... I think you're a lady.

Valerie (*laughing*) Yeah, and you're crackers.

Tom You gave me some tea from your flask, didn't you?

Valerie *That* doesn't make me a lady.

Tom It makes you ... kind. Caring ... Ouch!

She starts to interrupt

Look, if I want to think of you as a lady then I'm going to. OK?

Valerie (*flattered*) OK. There! (*She has the splinter and shows it to him on the end of the pin*)

There is a clap of thunder, which sounds nearer this time

Valerie Oh God ... we're really in for it, aren't we? I can cope with thunder – it's lightning that frightens me. (*She returns the pin to the collar of her coat*)

Tom (*taking a step nearer her*) That's very feminine of you.

Valerie Are you mocking me?

Tom I wouldn't do that.

Valerie What are you doing then?

Tom I'm reminding you of how feminine you are.

Valerie Is Helen (*she turns to face him and realizes he's much nearer to her than before*) scared of lightning?

Tom I don't think so.

Valerie That's interesting. (*She eases past him and faces out front*)

Tom Why?

Valerie Women don't come any more feminine than her. What I'm saying is she isn't a bit like me, is she?

Tom (*picking up his tea again and sitting down on his box*) She's got more than one dress in her wardrobe, if that's what you mean.

Valerie I bet there isn't a pair of trousers in the house.

Tom Well, only mine.

Valerie (*laughing*) Yes, of course. (*Her laughter subsides. She spots the toothbrush*) What's this toothbrush doing here? (*She picks it up*) I haven't noticed it there before.

Tom Really.

Valerie I mean, it wasn't there yesterday.

Tom Oh, it was. Well, perhaps it wasn't exactly there – but it's been there for a few days.

Valerie And there's obviously a reason for that?

Tom Obviously.

Valerie But you're not going to tell me.

Tom It's only a bloody toothbrush.

Valerie It's not something you usually see in an allotment shed.

Tom I've seen funnier things, believe me.

Valerie You don't want to talk about it.

Tom You've got it.

Valerie Why leave it there then?

Tom I didn't ... deliberately.

Valerie It's pretty obvious I'd spot it.

Tom (*shouting*) Val ... Just ... leave it. OK?

Another roll of thunder. Valerie tosses the toothbrush back on to the shelf

Valerie (*after a slight pause during which she sits again*) What shall I cook for Alan's tea? He won't have eaten lunch which means he'll be starving when he gets home. Whatever it is it will have to be huge.

Tom looks at her

He's days all this week. (*Slight pause*) What are you having? What will Helen have on the table when you get home?

Tom *I* do most of the cooking. Didn't know that, did you?

Valerie I guessed.

Tom How?

Valerie No-one can spend time in the kitchen and keep nails like Helen.

Tom (*getting up and moving towards Valerie*) Her eyebrows are the same. And her skin and her lips and her toe-nails ... (*He hands her his empty cup*) She's just perfect in every detail. (*He faces her but rests his bottom on the wooden shelf underneath the window*)

Valerie Yes ... I suppose she's quite a catch.

Tom Would you like to look like her?

Valerie (*returning the cup to her bag and laughing*) Can you imagine those nails on me? It'll be like looking at a street lamp with a silk shade.

Tom You're always putting yourself down.

Valerie No – I can like something – admire it – but know when it's not right for me. Where's the paste?

Tom (*after a slight pause*) Pardon?

Valerie The toothpaste. Where is it?

Tom Ran out. Need to get more.

Valerie From the house?

Tom Or the shops. Whatever.

Valerie (*after a slight pause*) She's thrown you out, hasn't she?

Tom Don't be ridiculous. (*He turns away from her*)

Valerie You've gone, though. You're not with her, I mean.

(*Slight pause*) Am I right?

He doesn't answer. He collects the packets of seeds from the shelf and puts them into a drawer

OK, don't talk about it if you don't want to. But I am a good listener if you need one.

Tom I don't know what I need at the moment.

Valerie But I am right. You've been staying here in the shed, haven't you?

Tom (*turning to face her*) For the last couple of nights, yes.

Valerie Pretty serious then.

Another roll of thunder, further away this time. Tom sits on his box, leaning forward on his elbows. A pause

Look ... you've had a bust up with Helen and you've both probably said a lot of things you didn't mean. Buy her some flowers ... or a blouse or something. That'll sort everything out.

Tom Most men think it wonderful to have a wife like her. They've said it to me. She's ... very fanciable. She's not the run of the mill, I know. But she's not a lot of other things either.

Valerie She's just your type, Tom.

Tom How would you know my type?

Valerie You married her, for God's sake!

Tom It doesn't mean anything. I'm sure Alan isn't *your* type. Well, not anymore.

Valerie You're not going to try and tell me that your wife doesn't understand you, are you Tom?

Tom I didn't want to tell you anything.

Valerie (*standing*) Ah, but you did. I'm not dull, Tom. I'm not stupid. I might not have got half a dozen O levels but I know a bit about people. You didn't just happen to leave that toothbrush there. You wanted me to see it.

Tom Just like you wanted to wind me up about taking my coat over to Norman's?

Valerie (*after a slight pause before sitting down*) I don't know what you're talking about.

Tom (*after a slight pause*) She has a jealous streak.

Valerie Helen?

Tom Someone told her about you.

Valerie Told her what about me?

Tom That I let you become a member. That I allocated you a plot next to mine.

Valerie It was the only one available, wasn't it?

Tom That wouldn't matter to Helen.

Valerie She can't be jealous of *me*, Tom. I'm almost old enough to be her mother, for God's sake.

Tom No, you're not.

Valerie And look at me ... I'm a forty-two hip.

Tom It doesn't matter how old or what shape you are.

Valerie Helen said that?

Tom No, that was me. (*Pause*) I've told Helen there's nothing between us.

Valerie But she didn't believe you.

Tom shakes his head

(*After a slight pause*) I think I should go and see her.

Tom No.

Valerie Not now. In a day or two. After the dust has settled.

Tom There's no point. She believes you don't have a thing for me.

Valerie What's the problem then?

Tom She thinks *I* have a thing for you.

Valerie starts to laugh. It grows until she can hardly control herself

Come on – share the joke.

Valerie Exactly. I've never heard anything so funny in my life. Helen is a very attractive woman, Tom. Very attractive. It's incredible to think you'd find me the same. (*She laughs again*)

Tom But I do.

Valerie's laughter fades

I think you're a real woman.

Valerie What does that make Helen?

Tom A doll. A very expensively dressed doll.

Valerie Oh, bugger off – she's more than that.

Tom No, she's not. Not to me. And hasn't been for a long time.

Valerie How long?

Tom Way back.

Valerie Before I joined the gardening club?

Tom Oh yes, long before then.

Valerie Does Helen know that?

Tom She knows it now.

Valerie Because you've told her?

Tom That was one of the many things we said to each other.

Valerie What else did you say to each other, Tom?

Tom I told her how I feel about you.

Valerie You told her ... I don't believe this.

Tom And that I know you like me too.

Valerie Oh you did —

Tom You do, don't you?

Valerie What woman in her right mind wouldn't?

Tom Val. (*Slight pause*) I've always been attracted by you.
Since the beginning I've felt ... well that there was some sort
of chemistry, you know? Then a couple of days ago I ... I just
couldn't go home to watch Helen dry her nails. And I use the
word home in the loosest possible sense. Our house isn't a
home anymore, it's a show piece. I bet we paid more for our
lounge curtains than you did for your car.

Valerie It isn't a very expensive car.

Tom You know what I mean. She's turned it into some sort of
shrine. All done out in pastel shades and cream carpets and
she's displayed all this artificial fruit in a nine and a half
thousand pound kitchen that I don't think she's ever been in
more than twice. It's like a bloody Barratt show house. (*Slight
pause*) Can you understand what I'm trying to say?

Valerie (*after a slight pause*) If you want to leave Helen, Tom, that's your business. But having a lovely house is hardly grounds for divorce.

Tom Now you're making fun of me.

Valerie What else am I supposed to do? (*Slight pause*) I think you're confused.

Tom I'm not confused about how I feel.

Valerie Well, I'm confused. Look at me, for God's sake. I can't believe you find me attractive.

Tom Alan did.

Valerie Have you seen Alan?

He doesn't answer her

No. He's over weight and has eczema. His table manners are nothing to be proud of and the only pastel coloured thing in our house is the toilet roll. We've been married twenty-nine years and he wasn't then and still isn't "a good catch" ... but neither was I. (*She corrects herself*) Am I. (*Slight pause*) I'm comfortable with him.

Tom So you love him?

Valerie He wouldn't have it any other way.

Tom (*firmly*) Answer me.

Valerie And neither would I.

Tom (*raising his voice*) Answer me!

Valerie (*shouting back*) I just did.

Pause. They look at each other and Tom eventually manages an uncomfortable smile. He gets up and goes to the door. Val watches him. He puts the clip down, locking it. He looks at Val as he inches towards her

Tom Look .... (*He puts his hand on her shoulder*) Why don't we —

Valerie No. Please, Tom ... no.

Tom (*trying to put his arm around her*) Why don't we we just —

Valerie (*getting up and moving* DR) No, don't touch me. Please!

Please, Tom. I'm very flattered ... but I thought we had something special.

Tom (*following her*) We have.

Valerie No, we haven't. (*Slight pause*) You've been flirting with me all this time and I didn't even know.

Tom I didn't read you wrong, Val. You flirted with me too.

Valerie Tom, I haven't flirted with anyone since I was a thirty-four bust. Youth club days. (*She crosses in front of him and moves* DL)

Tom When I helped you turn over your plot – showed you how to rake it – how to trench your potatoes and so on —

Valerie I thought you were being nice.

Tom You enjoyed all that as much as I did. Tell me you didn't try getting it wrong just so as I'd have to come and show you all over again. Go on – tell me. (*Insisting*) Tell me.

Valerie All right, I enjoyed it. But no more than if Norman or anyone else had shown me.

Tom Why don't I believe that?

Valerie I'm still not convinced that this isn't some kind of a wind-up. (*a slight pause*) When you gave me all those cabbage plants, carrot and beetroot seed —

Tom I'd have probably given them to anyone who happened to have the plot next to me at the time ... it's true. *Now* I'd give them to you for a totally different reason. (*He stands very close to her with both hands on her shoulders. He turns her round to face him*) Say something.

Valerie Why me?

Tom Why not? (*Slight pause*) All right, you're the first to admit you're no oil painting, right? OK, maybe it's true that no-one under normal circumstances would look twice at you —

Valerie I never said that.

Tom Didn't you? (*He thinks about it*) Anyway ... I've had the chance to look at you a lot more than that. I've got to know you ....

Valerie No-one has ever fancied me before ... apart from Alan and I don't want to hurt him.

Tom I understand that. But if you'll only give me a chance ...

Valerie Go home, Tom. Tell Helen all you've told me. Tell her everything.

Tom I'm not going anywhere until you tell me you don't feel anything for me.

Valerie I don't feel anything for you.

Tom (*shouting as he turns away from her to sit down on his box*) Why are you doing this?

Valerie For you! I'm doing it for you. (*She moves a little nearer to him*) Don't you see it would be the easiest thing in the world to say yes to you. (*She realizes what she has blurted out and is so annoyed with herself she mouths the word "shit"*)

Tom (*after a slight pause; looking up at her*) So you do like me?

Valerie I hate you for making me say it.

Tom And for making you feel like you do?

Valerie I'm never going to find myself in a situation like this again. I know that. Most women of my age .. (*She looks at him then moves away* DL) You're making it very difficult for me.

Tom (*going to her*) Then let me make it easier

Valerie No ... I don't want you to ... Tom ... please ... I —

He cups her face in his hands and kisses her very gently

Tom Now tell me you wish I'd never done that.

Valerie If you don't kiss me again I —

He kisses her again, a proper embrace this time. After a time they stop and she looks up into his eyes

Tom You're so beautiful.

Valerie Don't say that! (*She turns away from him*) I'm not used to that.

Tom Then you'd better get used to it. (*He tries to turn her towards him again*) What is it? What's the matter?

Valerie (*after a slight pause, quietly*) I'm scared.

Tom Of Alan?

She shakes her head

Helen?

Valerie Of how I feel. How you made me feel.

Tom (*flippantly*) And that was just a kiss.

Valerie (*snapping*) It's not funny.

Tom I'm sorry. (*Slight pause*) I feel the same too.

Valerie You don't – it's different for you.

Tom No it's not it's —

Valerie I still love Alan.

Tom In spite of everything?

Valerie Ironic, isn't it? But you don't stop loving somebody just because they've turned into a slob.

Pause. Neither really knows where to go from here

Tom What do you want to do?

Valerie I don't know. I've never been in this position before. Do people normally do what they want?

Tom I'm going to.

Valerie Which is what?

Tom Well, I've done it. I've left Helen.

Valerie (*crossing* R) But that's not fair. You've had time to work things out. You've sprung this on me.

Tom Oh, come on ... it's not as sudden as you're trying to make out.

Valerie (*turning to face him*) I didn't know you and Helen had split up.

Tom I was talking about how you felt about me. And *how* you feel has got nothing to do with me and Helen.

Valerie (*after a slight pause*) It still scares me.

Tom Only because you feel vulnerable.

Valerie That's right. I do feel vulnerable and I'm not sure I like it.

Tom You liked the rest of it, didn't you? It's a small price to pay.

Valerie I don't want an affair.

Tom I'm not offering you one. What I want from you isn't a quick grope and a screw in a garden shed. I just want to be with you. All the time. I thought I made that clear.

Valerie You did. (*She moves away* DL) You made yourself perfectly clear. (*She now stands just in front of the door*) It's me. I'm the problem.

Tom Look. (*He turns to face her*) Just think about this for a minute, right?

He goes to her. She leans against the inside of the door

If you're seriously considering me and we've only kissed, imagine ... (*He rests his arm on the wall above her head*) Imagine how it would be if ... all our problems would go away completely if we made love.

Valerie (*not threatened anymore, even managing a sort of a sexy smile*) You reckon?

Tom (*smiling back very close to her*) You want to do it, I know you do.

Valerie You're the devil on my shoulder, you know that, don't you?

Tom So what do you say?

Valerie (*after a slight pause*) You're a lovely looking bloke, Tom. I can't believe my luck – honest I can't ...

Tom Make love to me then. (*He grabs her and turns her around*) Let's hold each other and make the world go away. If only for twenty minutes.

Valerie That's great. That sounds wonderful, that does. There's only one thing wrong with it. Sooner or later the world is going to come back. And when it does it'll never be the same again.

Tom So what if you're not happy with the way things are?

Valerie I haven't said I'm not happy. All right, so I've got a dull marriage, and yes, there have been times when I've thought I'd like some excitement in my life and ... and, lo and behold here it is ... on a plate. Well, in a shed, anyway. (*Slight pause*) You're very fanciable too, Tom, but the thought of something happening between us was just a dream for me. It's not supposed to happen.

Tom What about *my* dream?

Valerie Keep it in your head. It's the best place for it. (*Slight pause. She moves away to get her coat*) I'm going now to cook lunch for Alan. He's having boiled ham, tinned potatoes, tinned carrots and frozen peas. He'll settle for that.

Tom What about you?

Valerie (*putting her coat on*) I reckon it'll do for me too.

Tom (*slight pause*) You're turning me down then.

Valerie Incredible isn't it? I can't believe I'm doing it myself.

Tom Look, just give me a chance ...

Valerie Believe me, Tom ... you came this close. (*She shows him with her thumb and index finger. Slight pause*) Take care of my plot?

Tom No. No, you don't have to do that.

Valerie It shouldn't be difficult for you. You did most of it anyway.

Tom You haven't got to give it up.

Valerie It's different now. It's not the same anymore.

Tom But we didn't do anything.

Valerie We wanted to. And that's just the same.

Tom Look, you love that thirty square yards. I can't take it from you.

Valerie You're not taking it. I'm giving it to you.

Tom (*after a slight pause*) What will you tell Alan?

Valerie Oh, that's easy. I'll just say he was right ... that I gave up .... that he won.

Tom (*turning away from her*) No freezer then.

Valerie No point. (*Slight pause*) I'll see you. (*She picks up her bag and opens the door*)

Tom Val?

Slight pause. She stops at the door with her back to him. He turns to face her

Alan's not there.

She doesn't answer

He's days all this week. (*Slight pause*) You couldn't have forgotten. (*Slight pause*) Val?

She closes the door then turns round to face him

Valerie (*after a long pause*) Oh, what the hell.

They embrace each other in a long, lingering kiss as the Lights fade to Black-out

CURTAIN

FURNITURE AND PROPERTIES LIST

On stage: General gardening equipment
     Tea-chest
     Tin barrel containing a cluster of bean sticks
     Tom's coat (wet)
     Large box
     Pot
     Shelves
     Plastic cups with runner beans
     Seed packets
     Small transistor radio
     Toothbrush
     Tube of toothpaste (used)
     Piece of sandpaper
     Lump of carved wood

Off stage: Bag. *In it:* flask of tea, two cups, two pasties
     wrapped in paper bags (**Valerie**)

Personal: **Valerie:** safety pin (in coat lapel)

LIGHTING PLOT

Interior. Same setting throughout
No practical fittings required

To open: Bring up rainy spring morning effect

Cue 1   **Tom** and **Valerie** embrace each other   (Page 19)
           Fade to black-out

EFFECTS PLOT

Cue 1   As the Curtain rises   (Page 1)
            Rather loud thunderclap; music; Tom
            Jones singing "It's Not Unusual",
            gradually moving from the auditorium
            into the transistor radio. Cut when
            Tom *turns off radio*

Cue 2   **Valerie** shows **Tom** the splinter   (Page 7)
            Louder thunderclap

Cue 3   **Tom**: "Just ... leave it. OK?"   (Page 9)
            Thunderclap

Cue 4   **Valerie**: "Pretty serious then."   (Page 10)
            Thunderclap (further away than before)

Printed by John Good Holbrook